Playing in the Zone

EXPLORING THE SPIRITUAL DIMENSIONS OF SPORTS

Andrew Cooper

SHAMBHALA   BOSTON & LONDON   1998

Shambhala Publications, Inc.
Horticultural Hall
300 Massachusetts Avenue
Boston, Massachusetts 02115
http://www.shambhala.com

9 8 7 6 5 4 3 2 1

First Edition
Printed in the United States of America
♾ This edition is printed on acid-free paper that meets
the American National Standards Institute Z39.48 Standard.
Distributed in the United States by Random House, Inc.,
and in Canada by Random House of Canada Ltd.

Library of Congress Cataloging-in-Publication Data

Cooper, Andrew, 1953–
    Playing in the zone: exploring the spiritual dimensions of sports/
Andrew Cooper.—1st ed.
        p.   cm.
    Includes bibliographical references (p.   ).
    ISBN 1-57062-151-9 (alk. paper)
    1. Sports—Psychological aspects.   2. Spirituality.   3. Sports—
Social aspects.   I. Title.
GV706.4.C67   1998   98-5799
796'.01—dc21   CIP

For Liz, my love
"I have come into my garden"

There are more things in heaven and earth, Horatio,
Than are dreamt of in your philosophy.   HAMLET

There have been only two geniuses in the world. Willie
Mays and Willie Shakespeare.   TALLULAH BANKHEAD

Contents

Introduction

For everything that lives is holy, life delights in life.
                                                WILLIAM BLAKE

The old baseball hand Wes Westrum once said, "Baseball is like church. Many attend, but few understand." Apply this point not just to baseball but to sport in general and you have, in a nutshell, the subject of this book.

In framing his analogy, Westrum might well have used another example. Any field of human endeavor requiring sophisticated and loving appreciation would do—Impressionist painting, jazz, Shakespearean drama—the list is endless. But he chose religion, and whatever his intent may have been, the choice is altogether proper. Although sport is a most secular activity in a highly secularized world, in its ability to provoke wonder, to elicit deep feeling, to grace our lives with glimpses of timeless beauty and freedom—in these and other ways sport is, though not religion, something religious.

This claim finds support in both history and experience. Like drama, music, and poetry, the beginnings of sport go back to the religious rites of the ancient world. Indeed, most sports popular today are derived from games played in ancient and medieval times, and through most of human history, before modern times, sport has maintained some explicit connection with its sacred origins. Though it is for the most part forgotten, that link is present still today—unseen, unspoken, and unconscious.

In this book I refer to this hidden dimension of sport as its *secret life*. I have borrowed the term from the novelist and essayist Colin Wilson, who himself borrowed it from the British playwright Harley Granville-Barker. For Wilson, the secret life is a realm of inner experience beyond the constraints of the ego's habits of perception. Though it is obscured by the narrow focus of our everyday consciousness, the secret life is the ever-present support on which that consciousness rests. It is, in T. S. Eliot's words, "the Life we have lost in living." We catch a glimpse of the secret life in what Wilson calls those "curious moments of inner freedom," in which we become so absorbed in the task at hand that the self is forgotten and experience is displayed in its primal power and pristine clarity. Sport provides such moments generously, and in our society, it does so more than perhaps any other single activity.

The secret life is closely connected with what the religious historian Mircea Eliade referred to as the "discovery of the sacred," an experience in which one perceives the difference between "what reveals itself as being real, powerful, rich, and meaningful and what lacks these qualities." In Eliade's view, sacredness and the drive to experience it are innate aspects of human nature. The sacred is often recognized through religion, but it is not defined by religion. The forms and symbols that express sacredness vary widely, but the inner movement toward it is a constant.

The secret life can be thought of as religion as it emerges from the depths of the self. Not the personal self, the ego, but the self that is one's identity when all ideas about identity are transcended. In the secret life, doctrines and institutions must rest on the foundation of experience. Their purpose is to serve the processes of transformation through which consciousness is enriched, broadened, and deepened, and by which it finds its own sacred ground. Throughout history, those who have pursued the secret life have often employed terms such as *esoteric meaning, inner essence, core teachings*, and the like to speak of its relationship to conventional religion. In other words, the secret life is not a matter of belief. Entry to it requires the appropriate cultivation and refinement of consciousness. It is indeed hidden, but the one doing the hiding is none other than oneself.

For the purposes of this book, I've taken a universalist approach to the secret life. That is, I've not used a particular spiritual tradition as a primary framework. While this was necessary, it is not without problems. Universal approaches to the inner life tend toward superficial eclectism, blandness, and distortion, as important distinctions are blurred and symbols, ideas, and practices are removed from the organic context in which they are rooted.

But my concern here is not with the secret life as it is revealed in religion but with how it is revealed in sport. And from that perspective, sport possesses a universal quality. The ball games of the pre-Columbian Mayans were fertility rites, in which the ball represented the life principle that was renewed through the playing of the game. For medieval German monks, such as Martin Luther, the game of *Kegels* (an antecedent of bowling) was a way to cleanse oneself of sin by using a ball to knock over the "devil." Today, George Will sees baseball as embodying the virtues of the secular religion of capitalist democracy, while for Fidel Castro the same game demonstrates the principles of his own religion of state socialism. *How* we interpret sports varies; *that* we interpret them does not. The many meanings we assign to sport are all embraced by a larger pattern. Sports are not limited by any single meaning; they are, rather, a source of meaning itself. By stirring deep feeling and imagination, they compel us to see reflected in them the truths of life. In this regard, sport is akin to myth: both draw us into a separate world and ask that we make an intelligible connection between that world and the one of everyday experience.

Sport is like myth, it is like religion, and it is like other things as well—art and war, to name two with which we will be particularly concerned. And sport extends beyond the playing field into other realms—business, politics, and other social institutions. But sport is *sui generis*, a class of activity unto itself. It is a basic category of human experience, irreducible and universal. Sport can be likened to many things, and many things can be likened to sport. Indeed, one mark of its significance is indicated by how widely we draw upon sport for the metaphors and themes that shape our cultural and personal lives. But sport is itself a distinct realm of human experience.

This distinctiveness is often lost on those who write about the spiritual and psychological dimensions of sport. Clearly techniques, principles, and perspective from, say, Zen Buddhism can be productively applied to enhance a player's performance or to enrich a spectator's appreciation. I shall certainly be concerned with such matters in what follows. But in addressing points of convergence, it is essential to preserve difference as well. This is not a Zen-of-tennis book. Zen is Zen, and tennis is tennis. Neither needs to be reduced to or justified by the terms of the other. It would be a mistake to collapse all distinctions, for each realm of experience must be seen from within its own perspective—its goals, purposes, history, social function, and guiding symbols. We learn as much by difference as by similarity. As Heraclitus said, "Different elements make the finest harmony."

Though we can differentiate sport from other activities, exactly what sport *is* is hard to define. The word itself comes from *disport*, "to divert or amuse," which is derived from the Latin *des porto*, "to carry away." Sports surely do provide pleasure by carrying us away from everyday concerns. But they do much more than that. They carry us out of ourselves and cast us into a larger world; they propel us into the presence of powers that are greater than the self yet in which the self is rooted.

While etymology reveals something of the meaning of sport, it doesn't define it. And, really, definition is beside the point. Were this a scientific inquiry, we would need an operational definition. But this is a book about experience, and so the semantic territory must be marked out in a manner consistent with experience. In our everyday use of language we are nowhere near as precise or consistent as are dictionary or experimental definitions. To our general sense of a word's meaning we apply intuition, a sense of context, personal idiosyncrasy, and so forth. Our meanings slip and slide and move off into streams of association.

To talk about what is meant by *sport*, we might picture the word at the center of a cluster of related, yet distinguishable, words and ideas. Sport is connected to play, but not all play has the formal quality of sport. Sport usually entails competition, but not always: golf, surfing, and skiing are sports whether or not they are performed competitively. Other words lie close to the cluster's center. *Athletics* and *contest*, for example, are related yet not the same. In addition, individual sports differ among themselves in how they embrace the various associations and how they highlight the differing qualities. The realm of sport may be distinct, but it has permeable and shifting boundaries.

The word most closely connected with sport, and thus the one most necessary to distinguish from it, is *game*. The philosopher Paul Weiss points out that one of the differences between the two terms is that sport entails history and memory. Today's box score tells of last night's game between the Braves and Reds. But when we speak of baseball as a sport, we mean more than a single instance of its playing. We mean something that has evolved over long years in countless enactments. There is something cumulative about a sport. But it is much more than that. A sport is a repository of tradition, lore, aspiration, and craft. The power with which sport reaches inward to the self is bound up with its power to reach backward to the past.

Another distinguishing mark of sports—at least for our purposes here—is that they involve players and spectators. Books on the inner aspects of sport tend to focus solely upon and give preference to the actual playing of the game. Spectating is considered to be a passive activity. The dichotomy is often a false one, as most people who enjoy watching sports also enjoy playing them. Furthermore, spectating can—indeed, should—be a participatory activity with its own demands. As with art or religion, the rewards of attending a sporting event depend on one's ability to enter imaginatively into the activity, and this requires knowledge, loving appreciation, and the ability to see beneath the level of one's hopes and expectations to the pure, intrinsically joyous form that is struggling to find expression. From the point of view of the secret life, player and spectator are but different perspectives contained within a single story.

The thirteenth-century Zen master Dōgen Kigen spoke of the progression of spiritual life as being like a spiral. In contrast to the linear, systematic metaphor of a path, the spiral more accurately reflects the tendency in inner life to revisit essential themes, illuminating them with greater vision and from new perspectives. In structuring this book I've kept in mind this spiral metaphor. Rather than develop a systematic approach to the inner world of sport, I've tried to find themes, ideas, and insights that would lead further into that world, and then to follow them.

In researching this book, I have cast a wide net. I have borrowed freely—and I hope responsibly—from the insights of others. At times there may be a clash of perspectives. This is necessary, because no single perspective is adequate for the subject. It may even be desirable, for new insights emerge from the creative tension of contradiction. To quote Heraclitus again: "That which opposes fits."

Since this is not a scholarly treatise, I've dispensed with the usual academic style of citation. As much as possible, I've tried to credit substantive contributions in the text itself. And I have, of course, included a bibliography at the book's conclusion.

In the theater of sport, the totality of our nature is given dramatic form. Sport displays the range of our experience in all its multiplicity, conflict, and contradiction. Human experience cannot be reduced to a single purpose or principle, and so neither can sport. In sport, as in the rest of life, appreciating complexity is a source of endless delight.

Through drama, metaphor, and symbol, sport speaks to us of our deepest yearnings and imaginings. Although our culture has undergone what Saul Bellow calls a "housecleaning of belief," we possess an irreducible need to resonate mythically with ourselves and with our world. Sport has always spoken to that need. It still does today, though we have, to a great extent, forgotten the language. When the primal significance of sports goes unrecognized, they are mere husks of what they can be and what they always have been. And what, in fact, they still, truly, are.

CHAPTER ONE

A Compelling Question

There comes a time in every man's life, and I've had plenty of them. **CASEY STENGEL**

Some moments live in memory as though they have their own secret tendency, as though they possess their own intention to perform some work on the self.

Years ago, I sat on the floor across a low, polished wood table from my Zen master, Taizan Maezumi Rōshi, both of us absorbed in translating a revered text by the great Zen ancestor Dōgen Kigen. Sipping green tea to warm us against the winter morning chill, we worked slowly and with great care. In Zen circles, Dōgen's writings are held to be among the most subtle and profound in all Buddhist literature, and they do not give up their meanings easily. Word by word, Rōshi led me into the world of the text, and I was enthralled by the elegance with which he disclosed its richness.

As we worked through the morning, I was scarcely aware of the passage of time, or even of the intense ache in my knees from hours of kneeling, Japanese-style, on the floor. Noticing the sun breaking through the late-morning haze, I was filled with a gracious sense of that intimate meeting of minds that is at the heart of Zen practice.

I had come from New York to the Zen Center of Los Angeles to immerse myself in Zen practice under Rōshi's guidance. He had come there from Japan to establish a center dedicated to transmitting the tradition to Westerners. But over the years, our common ground had grown increasingly elusive, as our many differences came to the fore. It felt good to get past our troubles for a while and to touch again what lay at the core of our relationship. The morning sparkled a bit more for it.

Our absorption was broken by a knock on the door. Charlotte, Rōshi's assistant, stepped in to inform me that there was an important phone call for me from Paul, a friend and fellow Zen student. This was odd. It was understood that interrupting Rōshi's meetings was not a casual matter. As one of the most senior students, Charlotte knew this well, as did Paul. I asked Charlotte to tell Paul that our meeting was nearly over and that I would call back promptly. A few moments later, she returned, saying that Paul insisted on speaking to me right away. Curious, and a bit annoyed, I asked what could be so urgent that it couldn't wait ten minutes. Charlotte replied, evasively, that I should just come to the phone.

Had I been focused less on Dōgen and more on the conversation, I would have been able to read the conspiratorial signals indicating that this was a matter best taken up outside Rōshi's ken. Instead, I pressed the issue and, given no choice, Charlotte said that Paul had been offered free tenth-row tickets to that night's Lakers-Sixers game and needed to know right away if I could go.

There is a Zen saying: When you walk, walk fully; when you run, run fully; above all, don't wobble. Good advice, but as I sat there, pulled one way by Master Dōgen, pulled another by Magic Johnson, I wobbled mightily. My mind raced as I calculated variables, heard internal testimony from the two sides, weighed the merits of various excuses that might justify taking the tickets and skipping out of evening meditation. Try as I might, I could not come up with anything that would be convincing even to myself, let alone to Rōshi

A formal Zen training period like the one we were then doing is highly structured, and one should miss meditation sessions only with good reason. I was well aware that, in Rōshi's eyes (which I now sensed were burning holes in the back of my head), Laker games clearly did not qualify. I turned back to meet his gaze and saw not the stern look I had anticipated but a very different expression, one of bafflement. I had seen the expression on just a handful of occasions. It was reserved for those times when the behavior of his American students appeared to him so strange as to be incomprehensible. He hadn't a clue as to why this matter would cause me the slightest hesitation. With a start, I realized that he too was wobbling—wobbling fully perhaps, but wobbling nonetheless.

We held each other's gaze, now two strangers staring across a seemingly unbridgeable chasm. After a long moment things became clear, and I asked Charlotte to tell Paul I could not go to the game. The matter settled, we returned to Dōgen.

But the matter was not as settled as I thought. Two hours later, in the space between two thoughts, I found myself on the phone pleading with Paul for the other ticket. I was in luck. That night, I slinked off to the Forum. It was a great game.

Back at the center after the game, sleepless from a giddy blend of guilt and elation, I reflected on the day's events. It occurred to me that the chasm that had loomed between Rōshi and me was also a chasm within myself. Two parts of myself, both rooted firmly and deeply, were strangers to one another. Both exerted powerful claims on my being, though the nature of these claims and the ways they made themselves felt were very different indeed. But the most striking difference was in my conscious relationship to them.

I regarded the spiritual impulse to be a fundamental human imperative, and I saw the refinement and cultivation of it as something with intrinsic and self-evident value. Through a practice such as Zen, this impulse was made explicit in activity and linked to a tradition of guidance, insight, and inspiration. Through practice, one joined a centuries-old conversation about what is most essential in human experience. And within the framework of that conversation, the purpose, meaning, and significance of practice is given the kind of rich elaboration that elicits and gives intelligibility to one's deepest intuitions.

The pull of sports was something else again. With the exception of a three-year post-1960s trial separation, they had been a constant in my life. Sports were just always there to be enjoyed. They were so close a part of daily life that I had rarely, if ever, paused to reflect on the power of their hold on me. I was an informed fan, fairly well read in sports literature, yet the source of my passion, even the idea of it, remained obscure. If I were asked to account for what it was that, in the words of the late A. Bartlett Giamatti (once the commissioner of Major League Baseball), held such a purchase on my soul, I would be hard pressed to answer. I simply did not have ideas that could do justice to the power of the experience.

We often don't immediately recognize an event's full significance until much later, after it has ripened through reflection and experience. Looking back on it now, the rather minor dilemma I encountered that morning at the Zen Center began a long process of exploration. Eventually that process led to the writing of this book.

A Matter of Faith

The French philosopher Paul Ricoeur observes that "enigma does not block understanding but provokes it." One finds this sensibility echoed in Zen Buddhism, especially in its tradition of koan study, where enigma is embraced, engaged, and appreciated as a generative source of insight. However one may approach it, to do the work of bringing wisdom, an enigma must provoke a recognition, however unformed, that it is a matter with existential import. We sense in it something of significance, even if we don't yet know its name.

Our lives seem to turn on such compelling questions. They may announce themselves suddenly or may incubate many years before we are even aware of their hold on us. They find their way into some deep region of the self and fasten themselves there. They irritate and inspire, frustrate and delight, all the while drawing one's attention like a magnet.

A compelling question resists easy answers. It requires tolerance—even appreciation—of uncertainty, ambiguity, and contradiction. One may dwell within it or circle around it for years, perhaps a lifetime, illuminating it first from one angle, then another. Such a question asks not just for concepts but for the kind of resonant knowledge that strikes a responsive chord within oneself, knowledge that brings a sense of rightness, as when one is caught up in an aesthetic moment. And though it is felt as intensely personal, over time the question connects one with life's perennial themes.

Over the years, my love of sports—our love of sports—has ripened into just this sort of question. What began as a *problem* of self-understanding became in time a *source* of self-understanding. It may sound strange to speak this way about so mundane a subject. At times the pursuit has certainly felt strange. And that fact, in itself, is most significant. We have relegated sports to the realm of entertainment. We speak of them as the toy department of life: diversions from matters of consequence, distractions from life's oppressive realities. Despite the immense amounts of time, money, energy, and intelligence our society invests in them, we have produced remarkably little in the way of serious thought about what they mean.

In his autobiography, *Second Wind: Memoirs of an Opinionated Man*, the basketball legend Bill Russell tells us, "There is no philosophy of sports worth mentioning," and this lack is the source of confusion and uncertainty for many a professional athlete. But its effects are not limited to professionals.

One most worthy exception to Russell's observation is Paul Weiss's *Sport: A Philosophic Inquiry*. Like Russell, Weiss laments the paucity of ideas that shed light on what sports mean and why they mean so much. Sports elicit our devotion and enthusiasm to a degree and with a readiness that is rare among human activities. This has been true throughout history and across cultures. And so questions about the meaning of sports go to the core of human experience. Yet throughout Western tradition sport has rarely been treated as a topic worthy of serious consideration. Weiss attributes this to the role of the privileged classes in establishing the norms of learned discourse. For the privileged, "the popular could not be as philosophically important as the rare, solely because it was popular." For the most part, matters of import to the great unwashed— that is, to ordinary people—have been neglected.

Soon after the death of the great baseball writer Ring Lardner, F. Scott Fitzgerald expressed regret that Lardner had squandered his talent on "a boy's game with no more possibilities in it than a boy could master, a game bounded by walls which kept out novelty or danger, change or adventure. . . . However deeply Ring might cut into it, his cake had the diameter of Frank Chance's diamond." This was in 1933. Yet eight years earlier, in *The Great Gatsby*, Fitzgerald had written through his narrator, Nick Carraway, "The idea staggered me. I remembered of course that the World Series had been fixed in 1919 but if I thought of it at all I would have thought of it as something that merely *happened*, the end of some inevitable chain. It never occurred to me that one man could start to play with the faith of fifty million people." The faith of fifty million is, of course, no small piece of cake. But I doubt Fitzgerald saw the incongruity of the two perspectives, because, taken together, they embody the unconscious double-mindedness of our society's ideas about sports: yes, they are widespread and intensely felt objects of devotion and faith; no, they are not worthy of serious intellectual or imaginative exposition.

For those who love them, sports are indeed a matter of faith, or at least they should be. They are not important in the way medicine or politics or law are important. Their value stems from their being separate from the realm of practical affairs that we call real life. They require not belief but the suspension of disbelief—in a word, faith. In this regard, sports resemble narrative art, myth, and religious ritual. That is, they require that one give oneself over to a story in which the elements of human experience are distilled, displayed, and integrated into a pattern of meaning that stirs the heart and quickens the soul. Sport creates a second world in which our deepest potentialities, our virtues and our vices, are revealed and cultivated within an order that raises them to beauty. One leaves the self's familiar confines to be enriched by other modes of experience. Those who believe in the importance of sports and those who believe in their triviality are equally mistaken. In matters of faith, such beliefs are beside the point.

The religious nature of sport is the subject of Michael Novak's *The Joy of Sports*, a work to which the present one is much indebted. Novak argues, eloquently and persuasively, that in American society sport is a kind of "natural religion":

> I am saying that sports flow outward into action from a deep natural impulse that is radically religious: an impulse of freedom, respect for ritual limits, a zest for symbolic meaning, and a longing for perfection. . . . I don't mean that participation in sports, as athlete or fan, makes one a believer in "God," under whatever concept, image, experience, or drive to which one attaches the name. Rather, sports drive one in some dark and generic sense "godward."

Sports satisfy our deep hunger to connect with a realm of mythic meaning, to see the transpersonal forces that work within and upon human nature enacted in dramatic form, and to experience the social cohesion that these forms make possible. Whether or not we so name them, these are religious functions. But our society so thoroughly secularizes sport that we can barely recognize, let alone express, what it makes us feel. Sport is, in Novak's words, "a faith without explanation." There is, however, something inherently unsatisfying about such a state of affairs. As theologians of the Middle Ages knew, faith calls out for exposition: *fides quarens intellectum,* faith in search of understanding, is a necessary movement of the soul. With the need left largely unmet, our innermost sensibility about sport remains vague and incomplete.

The historical record substantiates Novak's argument about sport's religious nature. Our ancient ancestors believed sport was a gift of the gods, something with divine purpose. Sport has its beginnings in religious rites performed to win favor with the gods, to placate unseen powers,to honor departed heroes. Most importantly, they were a form of fertility magic. The ball games of native America, the wrestling matches of West Africa and Japan—these and other forms of ritual contest among ancient peoples were created to expedite the passing of the seasons, to bring rain, and to ensure abundant harvests.

Ancient Greece was, of course, the site of an extraordinary flourishing of sacred sport. For more than a thousand years, festivals combining religious ceremony, cultural pageantry, and athletic competition were essential features of Greek society. Hundreds of local festivals were conducted annually throughout Greece and its colonies. Major festivals, such as the Olympic Games, drew huge crowds of spectators and contestants from near and far and were a focal point of cultural life.

For the Greeks, athletic contests were offerings to the gods. They were surrounded by ceremony and celebrated in poetry. Within this sacred context, sport was a container in which aggressive passions were channeled and transformed and an arena in which virtues were cultivated and displayed. Participation in sport, whether as contestant or spectator, was seen as an activity that educated, enriched, and emancipated the soul.

But sport is, by its nature, something that can be enjoyed for its own sake. Over the centuries, this function has eclipsed its sacred one. Today we understand sport as an explicitly secular activity. Attempts at finding in it something of spiritual significance usually yield little more than simpleminded moral preachments or New Age nostrums. But the sacred currents run deep, and despite ourselves, we still feel their insistent pull.

Sports may no longer be about transcendence, but they still enact transcendence. They retain their power to intensify experience and awaken within us a larger sense of being. They continue to provide forms that make present to us the primordial forces that in other times were called gods, that today might be called archetypes, and whose narratives still constitute the primary themes of art, philosophy, and psychology. This is the hidden dimension of sport, its secret life.

The Purpose of the Playing

Athletes "live out human possibilities in ceremonial form," to borrow a phrase from the author Kevin Kerrane. With startling clarity, they display the spectrum of human experience. In this regard, sport serves a function similar to that which Shakespeare, in *Hamlet,* ascribed to theater: "The purpose of playing . . . is to hold, as 'twere, the mirror up to nature; to show virtue her own feature, scorn her own image, and the very age and body of the time his form and pressure." Art surpasses sport in the complexity, intelligence, and imaginative power with which it can accomplish this. But the theater of sport, having no script and thus being further removed from human intentions, is tied more closely to chance, to karma, to destiny. Like life itself, a sport is a progression of quirks, surprises, and bizarre turns. No matter how mightily Hamlet grapples with his fate, it will always lead him to the same place. But the fate of the New York Mets—that is something even God must guess at.

Just as it was for our ancestors in antiquity, sport is magical. But sport's power to move us is as much a cause for concern as it is for celebration. Critics who rail against its pathologies are for the most part justified. It is a truism to say that the world of sport is a circus of greed, corruption, hypocrisy, and exploitation. Sports are indeed tools for the stimulation of frivolous appetites and base emotions. They provide a false sense of relief from the real problems of powerlessness, anonymity, and isolation that are imposed by our social institutions. They are a playground of distraction and childish regression. They are, despite considerable progress, rife with racism and sexism. Perhaps most perniciously, as Dr. Goebbels knew well, they can be used to inflame nationalist, ideological, and ethnic passions.

Sport is integrally connected with society. It is surely no cure for or escape from social ills. Indeed, in sport these ills are often magnified, as they are in other primary institutions, such as politics and religion. But most criticism of sport is less about sport than it is about the society of which it is a part. Such criticism is necessary for any realistic appraisal of the meaning of sport, but it is not sufficient. Sport is not reducible to social analysis.

Not only does sport reflect society, but our understanding of sport is to a great extent socially constructed, and thus it too reflects the virtues and shortcomings of society. As linguistic and anthropological study has shown, we make sense of experience through a network of meaningful forms that are culturally transmitted. In everyday experience, the deeper of these are premises that are largely unconscious and unexamined. Notions of fundamental meaning and value—the nature of the self, of good and evil, of sacred and profane, and the like—constitute what the religious historian Elaine Pagels calls "our mental architecture." Whether we consciously believe them or not, these ideas shape our experience. And so it is with sport. We understand sport within the framework of our cultural ideas. Today these ideas lack the imaginative scope that could give expression to the deep significance we sense is there.

The Jungian analyst Edward Edinger writes that mythology provides forms and categories by which the ego can develop a conscious relationship with the archetypal forces, or fundamental structures, of the psyche. Without such a relationship an individual will either be confined to a shallow level of experience or be subject to the unconscious and distorted manifestation of those deep psychic energies. And so it is with sport. Whether we deny them or not, sport's mythic undercurrents cannot be held back. Failure to grasp the deeper significance of sports deprives them of beauty, stunts our appreciation, and makes us vulnerable to what is worst in sport, and in ourselves. Not coincidentally, Edinger also cites the crucial role of athletics in ancient Greece, where they served a civilizing function by providing public forums in which primitive energies were contained and harmonized. To the degree that we allow, they do the same today. But it is to a far smaller degree.

It is a commonplace to say that ours is a society obsessed by sport, and I cannot imagine any reasonable person arguing the point. But there is more to it. Our obsession with sport is a signal of its value. It is but a distorted sign of our passion to realize such qualities as beauty, excellence, transcendence, freedom, and communion. The problem with our obsession is not that we care about sports too much but that we care too little. We delight in the thrills, but we don't love the craft. We draw simple moral lessons when what is being revealed is the complexity of human nature. We confuse price with value. We want technical mastery without appreciating the traditions through which such mastery is transmitted. We demand the satisfaction that winning brings while ignoring the meaning that winning confers. We consume sports like we consume Big Macs. And in so doing, the intrinsic joys and inner life are lost.

But the ills of sport can reveal the secret life even as they conceal it. The madness sports incite speaks of power poorly channeled, an indicator that they are now, as they were at the beginning, matters of primary import. Despite the nonsense and corruption that surround it, sport is, both historically and psychologically, an essential feature of human existence. Could we separate the wheat from the chaff, could we allow sport its proper measure and proportion, we would find, I think, that it deserves less than is indicated by our actions and more than is indicated by our thinking. We want so much from sport, but rarely do we consider that sport may want something of us.

The nineteenth-century literary critic Walter Pater asserted that the primary value of art lies in the inward experience of that reverie through which the mind enjoys its freedom. And so it is with sport. But the freedom conferred by both art and sport does not come without its demands.

To do its inner work, sport demands from the player the rigorous application of skill, intelligence, and creativity within the inherent designs of the game. From the spectator, it demands a knowledgeable and loving eye. From both, it requires a passion to know those moments when we glimpse that perfection of form that is always sensed yet never attained.

Pater is today best remembered for a single observation: "To burn always with this hard, gem-like flame, to maintain this ecstasy, is success in life." And so it is in sport. This gem-like flame is the gift sport bestows, the quality it requires, and the capacity it displays.

CHAPTER TWO

The Zone

When hungry, eat; when tired, sleep.

ZEN PROVERB

They throw the ball, I hit it. They hit the ball, I catch it.

WILLIE MAYS

Right away, you could see it was over. As he turned and headed back upcourt, Michael Jordan looked over at network announcer Magic Johnson and shrugged, as if to say, "It's beyond me. It's just happening by itself!"

It was the first game of the 1992 NBA finals, the Bulls against Portland. Michaelangelo had just sunk his sixth consecutive three-pointer, and in that moment it appeared as though even he was overwhelmed by the immensity of his gift. And that was the give-away. He had become self-conscious, and so he had lost that edge, that intensity of concentration in which limitations are forgotten and the spirit is set free to soar. But now the streak was over. Even for Michael Jordan, visiting hours on Olympus are limited.

Michael Jordan is no common athlete, and his shooting display was certainly no common feat. But for all its spectacle, his experience—its nature, its inner life—is not that unusual after all. Several miles and countless worlds away from Jordan's Chicago Stadium homecourt, a University of Chicago psychology professor, Mihaly Csikszentmihalyi, had recently gathered the results of twenty-five years of research into a book that sheds more light on Jordan's performance than you are likely to find on any sports page.

In *Flow: The Psychology of Optimal Experience*, Csikszentmihalyi sets forth his findings on the nature of human happiness, the matter that has been of primary interest throughout his professional life. What do people feel when they are most happy? What is their state of mind? Why do certain activities bring enjoyment and others do not? In investigating such questions, Csikszentmihalyi identified a dimension of human experience that is common to people the world over, regardless of culture, gender, race, age, or nationality. Elderly Korean women, Japanese teenage motorcycle gang members, Navajo shepherds, assembly line workers in Chicago, artists, athletes, surgeons—all described the experience in essentially the same words. Its characteristics include deep concentration, highly efficient performance, emotional buoyancy, a heightened sense of mastery, a lack of self-consciousness, and self-transcendence. Csikszentmihalyi calls the experience *flow*. Today's athlete calls it being in *the zone*.

The zone. I can't remember exactly when I first heard the term. It is a fairly new development in the lexicon of sports culture, perhaps fifteen years old, as near as I can tell. It denotes a place, as in the dictionary definition, but there is more to it than that. It calls up imagery of the supernatural ("the twilight zone") and carries an implicit connection to altered states of consciousness ("zoned out" or "lost in the ozone"), a connection made explicit by less popular related terms: "He was playing *out of his mind*." "She went *unconscious*." But *the zone*, with its rich ambiguity and layers of meaning, says it best. It is indeed a place, but a map won't get you there.

In *Every Goy's Guide to Common Jewish Expressions*, Arthur Naiman observes that Yiddish has an extraordinary number of words for a jerk—to wit: *shlemiel, nebbish, schlep, shlump, nayfish, zhlub, shmageggie,* and (my personal favorite) *yutz*—and we're just warming up. He compares this to the Eskimos having fourteen (or however many; I've heard various numbers) words for snow, noting that a language reflects the culture, environment, and needs of the people that speak it. (Of course, as Naiman says, it's clear why Eskimos would need so many words for snow, but it's anybody's guess why in Jewish culture this particular condition would require so varied and nuanced a descriptive arsenal.)

The emergence of a popular idiom indicates that a culture has come to recognize something previously unnamed as real and significant. The advent of the term *the zone* points to a growing awareness of the role of consciousness in sports. We are, as a culture, finally catching up to Yogi Berra, who long ago observed, "Ninety percent of hitting is mental. The other half is physical."

While the term is recent, the experience it points to is not. In his autobiography, *Second Wind*, written in 1979, Bill Russell evokes the "mystical feeling" that would on occasion lift the action on the hardwood to the level of magic.

> Every so often a Celtic game would heat up so that it became more than a physical or even mental game, and would be magical. That feeling is difficult to describe, and I certainly never talked about it when I was playing. When it happened I could feel my play rise to a new level. . . . At that special level all sorts of odd things happened. . . . It was almost as if we were playing in slow motion. During those spells I could almost sense how the next play would develop and where the next shot would be taken. Even before the other team brought the ball in bounds, I could feel it so keenly that I'd want to shout to my teammates, "It's coming there!"—except that I knew everything would change if I did. My premonitions would be consistently correct, and I always felt then

that I not only knew all the Celtics by heart but also all the opposing players, and that they all knew me. There have been many times in my career when I felt moved or joyful, but these were the moments when I had chills pulsing up and down my spine.

These spells were fragile. A bad call, a poor play, an injury, or some other minor disturbance might be enough to break the rhythm. When the spell broke, Russell always experienced a letdown, because there was nothing he could do to bring it back. Like grace, such moments came when they came, and all he could do was play his best and hope. But while in the midst of it, the sense was, "This is it. I want to keep this going."

In her autobiography, *Billie Jean*, the tennis great Billie Jean King describes the same territory.

> It's a perfect combination of . . . violent action taking place in an atmosphere of total tranquility. . . . When it happens I want to stop the match and grab the microphone and shout, *"That's* what it's all about." Because it is. It's not the big prize I'm going to win at the end of the match, or anything else. It's just having done something that's totally pure and having experienced the perfect emotion, and I'm always sad that I can't communicate that feeling right at the moment it's happening. I can only hope people realize what's going on.

As compelling as these experiences were, they were surrounded by a certain reticence. One hears in King a feeling of regret and frustration with the experience's elusiveness to language. Russell never spoke about the matter: "I felt a little weird about it, and quite private." The subject was taboo, and he knew that breaking that taboo would invite the mockery of his peers.

The situation has changed since Russell's playing days, but not all that much. Today "the zone" is a cliché for athletes and sports journalists. But its significance remains as elusive as ever. We hear all the time about someone being in the zone, but what does that really mean? If, as Russell, King, and others say, such moments are "what it is all about," what then can they tell us about the nature of sports and, indeed, of those who play them? What *is* it all about? And what is "it"? Certainly not just basketball or tennis. They are the means, doorways through which one passes, keys that unlock an inner experience.

Several years ago I discussed this with Scott Ostler, the prize-winning sports columnist for the *San Francisco Chronicle*. Ostler told me that he has tried on occasion to pursue the subject in some depth with athletes "only to be met with blank stares, like I was weird for asking." Perhaps the weirdest thing about the zone is how little is said about it.

But if those at the center of sports culture are reluctant to say much, a growing number at the periphery—writers, researchers, psychologists, and recreational athletes—are not. In a 1989 *New York Times Magazine* piece, Larry Shainberg reported that the zone has been investigated by psychologists, neurologists, and anthropologists, among others, and it has been explained in terms of genetics, environment, motivation, hypnosis, and even parapsychology. Sports psychologists, now fixtures in the high-pressure world of professional sports, commonly draw upon meditation and visualization techniques, the martial arts, and Western psychotherapy in devising programs intended to help their clients reach the zone more readily. On a popular level, the past fifteen years have seen the proliferation of books and articles offering advice on developing the inner aspects of golf, tennis, baseball, skiing, and so forth. While the quality of such publications varies, their popularity attests to the resonance of the theme they identify.

The former NFL linebacker David Meggyesy echoes Russell's view that the sports world is simply not a hospitable place to talk about experiences that are so intensely personal and out of the ordinary. Our culture lacks a rich vocabulary for describing the varied terrain of the inner world. Psychology, the field most concerned with inner experience, has throughout its history focused almost entirely on states of pathology. Until recently, it has had next to nothing to say about states that are of a higher order than normal waking consciousness.

Meggyesy says that the discourse of sports culture not only reflects this impoverished view; it magnifies it. (Remember Crash Davis tutoring Nuke LaLoosh in *Bull Durham* on the clichés of the basic postgame interview: "We gotta play 'em one day at a time." "I just want to give it my best shot.") In ways subtle and not so subtle, athletes are trained to keep their ideas within the safe confines of a small intellectual field. Besides, even the most distinguished speaker would have trouble describing deep personal experience in a sound bite.

The sports psychologist Rick Wolff says, "Ask a guy who just pitched a no-hitter how it felt, and he'll say, 'I don't know, but everything I wanted to do, I did.'" The sports writer Tim Keown compares an athlete's recognition of being in the zone with the way the Supreme Court recognizes pornography: "They can't explain it, but they know when they're in it."

Going Beyond

The more dramatic experiences of the zone can border on the ineffable. Our ordinary language is good at describing ordinary events, but how is one to speak of that which surpasses the bounds of the ordinary? That may be the province of poets; we have different expectations of our athletes. Nevertheless, for Meggysey, "The zone is the essence of the athletic experience, and those moments of going beyond yourself are the underlying allure of sport."

Meggysey regards the notion of the zone as a general concept, referring to a spectrum of experiences with varying characteristics and degrees of intensity. We tend to lump them all together under a single heading because we lack the vocabulary that would allow us to make the distinctions necessary for a more subtle and systematic understanding. Still, when taken together, these experiences exemplify an innate tendency for self-transcendence, and they reveal that, at their heart, sports are a way to unlock those hidden possibilities.

I first met David Meggyesy in 1992, and we hit if off right away. In researching this book, I wanted to include perspectives of some high-level athletes, and so I wrote to several dozen current and former professionals asking for their participation. Meggyesy was my one respondent. Not only was he willing to talk, he was excited by the prospect. I was not really surprised. I knew enough of his background to know that the different drum he has long marched to had led him down the road I now was exploring.

In 1970, at the height of his career with the Saint Louis Cardinals, Meggyesy quit professional football. Unlike most of his peers, his status as a professional athlete had not insulated him from the powerful social currents of the time. In his 1971 book, *Out of Their League*, he describes his struggle to reconcile the contradictory principles of the antiwar movement and counterculture with those of the big business of pro sports. *Out of Their League* is an angry book, a player's-eye-view indictment of the greed, corruption, and hypocrisy surrounding the game.

It is immediately obvious that the book pulls no punches. In his foreword, Meggyesy writes, "After playing the sport most of my life, I've come to see that football is one of the most dehumanizing experiences a person can face." The book describes the systematic exploitation of players, the league's pervasive racism, the malevolent spirit of the game's violence, and even the militaristic aura that attached itself to the game and attached the game to the war in Vietnam. As Meggyesy's involvement in the antiwar movement grew, and organizational pressure to keep his politics to himself intensified, he came to the point where it was "impossible for me not to see football as both a reflection and reinforcement of the worst things in American culture."

To say *League* struck a nerve would be an understatement. *Look* magazine serialized it, calling it "the roughest sports book ever written." Not wishing to add fuel to fire, NFL Commissioner Pete Rozelle issued a leaguewide gag order on the book and its author. Meggyesy recalls that the one prominent NFL figure to ignore the ignoring was Vince Lombardi, who pronounced Meggyesy something of a raving lunatic.

But countless others disagreed with Lombardi. *League*'s exposure of the underside of institutional athletics made it required reading in courses on many college campuses. As a matter of fact, Meggyesy came to speak at my own alma mater, Oberlin College, in 1973, my freshman year. Those were heady days, and even at a school as liberal as Oberlin, our athletic department was pretty far out. The program's director was the well-known sports activist Jack Scott, author of *The Athletic Revolution*. Second in command was Tommy Smith, winner of the gold medal in the 200 meters at the 1968 Olympics, whose clenched-fist salute on the winners stand during the national anthem still stands as one of that era's most potent images of black pride. The department offered courses with names like "The Role of the Athlete in Capitalist Society," "Sport and Racism," and "Body/Mind Harmony through Gymnastics." Counterculturally speaking, if it was happening anywhere, likely as not, it was happening at Obie sports.

With his shoulder-length hair, beard, jeans, and headband, Meggyesy fit right in. Even his size: he was certainly big for a professor or student or hippie, but for an NFL linebacker he seemed, well, kind of average. (Indeed, by NFL standards he was a bit undersized for his position.) At Oberlin and other campuses, and to thousands more through his book, Meggyesy spoke to those, like myself, who were trying to find a way to reconcile our love of sports with the skepticism that had emerged from the alternative perspectives of the 1960s. Meggyesy's story was our story writ large. It gave words to our feelings of confusion and discouragement. And if, in its bitterness, *League* did not provide a satisfactory resolution to the contradictions it names, by telling the story of his own struggles, Meggyesy clarified and validated the forces so many of us felt were at work in our own predicaments.

But Meggyesy was searching. While working on *League* he made his way down the California coast from Berkeley to Esalen Institute, in Big Sur. The world of encounter groups and hot baths on oceanside cliffs was as close to that of the NFL as it was to Mars, and the middle-class ethos of the scene was a long way from Meggyesy's blue-collar upbringing. Nevertheless, something clicked, some sense of a deep resonance between the explorations of human consciousness going on at Esalen and a kind of deep spirituality he had on rare occasions experienced in sports. And so, along with Esalen founder Michael Murphy, the author George Leonard, and several others, he founded the Sports Center at Esalen precisely to explore such connections. He's been exploring them ever since.

Today David Meggyesy is the West Coast representative of the NFL Players Association. The cramped bookshelves of his San Francisco office attest to the workings of a searching intelligence, whose interests range from contract law to Jungian psychology, with all stops in between. The worn-out jeans and headband have given way to a jacket and tie, at least when he's at work. In other ways, at fifty-two he looks pretty much the same as I remember him from more than twenty years ago: the same thick neck and firm jaw; the dark eyes under heavy brows that light up readily with the movements of an intense spirit.

Meggyesy is back in football, though he is still something of an outsider. As a union organizer, he operates on the fringes of the system. And that is just how he likes it. At our first meeting, he tells me he has just returned from "the combine," pro football's annual predraft camp, where college players are prodded, tested, examined, and measured to determine their "investment potential." "We [the Player's Association] meet with them to remind them that they are people, not just meat on the hoof, and to talk with them about the realities of the football business." After all these years and countless such gatherings of the football industry, "this one is still quite a circus."

As we make small talk to get acquainted, I mention the impression *League* had made on me years before. Meggyesy glances down, reflectively. "I was very angry back then, and the book gave me a way to express that anger. But it doesn't really show how much I loved the game." Though much has improved since his playing days, business as usual in the football industry is still anathema to what Meggyesy calls "the intrinsic satisfactions of the game." "But the thing is," he says, "you can't keep the magic down. It will always pop up, because those moments of pure, effortless intuition are what the game is really about."

But the problem is not merely the result of how football conducts its business. In Meggyesy's view, the greater problem is the broader culture's limiting ideas about sport. "The kind of experience athletes mean when they speak of the zone is like a diamond in a setting. Culture is the setting, and ours doesn't yet have the concepts that can hold and give adequate meaning to these experiences." To provide such a context would expand the horizons of what we understand sports to be about. But as it now stands, in our appreciation of sports' spiritual significance we are, like the man in the Polynesian adage, "standing on a whale fishing for minnows."

As a culture, we have come to associate profound experiences of our sense of being with religious contemplation, poetic revelry, or communion with nature. But, as Meggyesy insists, such experiences are extremely common in athletics. The passions they arouse, the demands they make, and the mental focus they require bring to bear our most exceptional inner resources. Despite our skepticism, athletics provoke us to magic.

To illustrate his point, Meggyesy recalls an exchange between Bill Moyers and the late scholar of world mythology Joseph Campbell in their now-famous PBS series of interviews, "The Power of

Myth." Moyers asks Campbell about Abraham Maslow's notion of *peak experiences*, which Campbell defines as those "moments in your life when you experience your relationship to the harmony of being." Campbell then says that his own such experiences all came in athletics. Campbell starred in track during his student days at Columbia, and when Moyers asks him to describe his own "Everest" among the peaks, Campbell recalls a meet in which he was to run the final leg in a relay. Though Campbell was far behind when he received the baton, he describes an exhilarating moment in which he was seized by an irrational certainty that he simply could not be beaten. And sure enough, he was right.

According to Meggyesy, not only are zone experiences common among athletes, but they become more common the higher the level of play. For those playing at the highest levels, the ability to put oneself in a state of heightened concentration—to get "psyched up," to "stay focused"—is as essential as physical ability, technical mastery, and knowledge of the game. Every so often, out of that concentrated state, a player's consciousness seems to make, of its own, a qualitative jump to a higher level. For someone like Campbell, who can fit such an experience into an overall view of life, it can have a powerful effect. But, says Meggyesy, most athletes (and most people in our culture in general) lack a supporting perspective that recognizes the significance of these experiences. They happen, they're great, and they're gone.

For several years in the early 1980s, Meggyesy taught classes at Stanford University focusing on the social and psychological aspects of athletic experience. Many of those attending played on school teams. Though many players were at first quite guarded about discussing their personal experiences, in time they came to feel comfortable about it. Meggyesy says he was struck by how frequently and enthusiastically class members spoke about the deep inner states they would sometimes enter and the exceptional ways they could perform while in those states. He came away from Stanford convinced that the psychology of athletic training is incomplete because, for the most part, it ignores this essential part of an athlete's experience. Like any aspect of experience, the exceptional abilities of athletes in the zone get stunted if they can't be talked about. Ironically, focusing just on what a player does and neglecting his or her inner experience may hinder the attainment of the highest levels of performance.

Peaks and Flows

Research findings give scientific support to Meggyesy's personal observation. Ken Ravizza, a professor of psychology at California State University at Fullerton, has long criticized the lack of focus on the subjective experience of athletes and has for years studied and written about peak experiences among athletes. In his article "Qualities of the Peak Experience in Sport," Ravizza writes:

> The peak experience in sport is a rare personal moment that
> remains etched in the athlete's consciousness. It serves as
> reminder of the great intrinsic satisfaction that sport participation
> can provide. Peak experiences during an athlete's career are rela-
> tively rare but their intensity acts as a standard, or qualitative refer-
> ence point, for subjectively evaluating future performance.

Ravizza describes three characteristics of an athlete's peak experience: focused awareness, complete control of self and environment, and transcendence of self. Based on his findings, Ravizza suggests that a greater sense of fulfillment may lead an athlete to a higher level of performance and that a better understanding of an athlete's state of consciousness when performing at an optimal level may indicate methods for enhancing performance.

In her doctoral dissertation, "Elite Athletes in Flow: The Psychology of Optimal Sport Experience," Susan Jackson used Csikszentmihalyi's notion of flow to explore the experience of twenty-eight world-class athletes, male and female, including a number of Olympic medalists. Jackson found that all her subjects agreed that the flow state was significant and influential in athletic pursuits. The majority went further, asserting that flow was necessary for the achievement of peak performance. In addition, all the athletes recognized that they could influence the achievement of the flow state through their own mental and physical preparation, though they also acknowledged that flow is subject to uncontrollable influences as well. Of the various characteristics of flow, those most relevant to the athletes were concentration, the merging of action and awareness, a feeling of mastery, and enjoyment of the activity for its own sake.

For our present purposes, Jackson's findings are especially noteworthy for two reasons. First, they indicate that optimal subjective experience is key in the enhancement of an athlete's performance. Even for elite athletes, such as those in Jackson's study, who receive considerable external reward, the enjoyment of playing the game for its own sake contributes to the quality with which the game is played. The other key point is that an athlete can do things to influence the achievement of such optimal experiences.

Later we will look more closely at what flow is and how it is achieved. But it is worth noting here that the research on it has already had consequences in the athletic world. A number of sports psychologists, trainers, and coaches have begun integrating the idea into their programs. Indeed, following the Dallas Cowboys' victory in the 1993 Superbowl, coach Jimmy Johnson credited Csikszentmihalyi's book *Flow* with helping him and his team prepare for the game. (I'd bet the farm that he neglected to leave a copy for Barry Switzer.)

Jackson found that most of her subjects had difficulty distinguishing between flow and peak experience. The problem arose in part because the two states share certain key characteristics. Another factor is that each state can be experienced with varying degrees of depth, and so their defining boundaries become fuzzy. But the biggest problem is one inherent in any attempt to make an experience the object of systematic, especially scientific, study.

Peak experience and *flow* are scientific terms, and as such they are precisely defined. But the terms refer not to material objects but to qualitative states of experience. Although an individual can define meticulously the qualities that characterize an experience, that does not guarantee that other individuals will not perceive and name that experience in different ways. Words carry an overlapping surplus of meanings, and these meanings are unfixed and dynamic. Furthermore, language is itself productive: it not only names our perceptions, but also shapes and evokes them. By scientific standards, the fit between language and experience is imprecise.

This is the problem Jackson ran up against when her subjects had a hard time distinguishing flow and peak experience. If such imprecision exists in a scientific situation, which is specifically designed to minimize it, we can be sure that it is far more pronounced in our everyday speech.

This can become a problem if we try to pin down too exactly the meaning of a colloquial term, such as *the zone*. The term is used widely in sports culture, but agreement about its meaning is only general. When it comes to specific details, there is plenty of room for interpretation.

In the Introduction I suggested that, rather than define sport, we think of it as lying at the center of a cluster of associated terms. We can approach the zone in a similar manner. An athlete who speaks of being in the zone is describing the experience of any of a number of qualities clustered around the term.

Many of the qualities of the zone are apparent in the passage quoted earlier in which Bill Russell describes the level of play he called magical: profound joy, acute intuition (which at times feels like precognition), a feeling of effortlessness in the midst of intense exertion, a sense of the action taking place in slow motion, feelings of awe and perfection, increased mastery, and self-transcendence.

Others who have described zone experiences have highlighted different aspects. Other than heightened performance, the quality mentioned most often is probably concentration. The British golfer Tony Jacklin, for example, would on occasion find himself in what he described as a "cocoon of concentration":

> When I'm in this state, this cocoon of concentration, I'm living fully in the present, not moving out of it. I'm aware of every inch of my swing. . . . I'm absolutely engaged, involved in what I'm doing at that particular moment. That's the important thing. That's the difficult state to arrive at. It comes and it goes, and the pure fact that you go out on the first tee of a tournament and say, "I must concentrate today," is no good. It won't work. It has to already be there.

Mentioned almost as frequently as concentration are calmness and confidence. In his autobiography, *My Life and the Beautiful Game*, the soccer genius Pelé recalls a day when he experienced "a strange calmness" unlike anything he had experienced ever before:

> It was a type of euphoria; I felt I could run all day without tiring, that I could dribble through any of their team or all of them, that I could almost pass through them physically. I felt I could not be hurt. It was a very strange feeling and one I had not felt before. Perhaps it was merely confidence, but I have felt confident many times without that strange feeling of invincibility.

Taken together, concentration, calmness, and confidence create a state of "relaxed concentration" that Jackson sees as nearly synonymous with the flow state. Furthermore, she found that the states most likely to disrupt flow were their opposites: inability to control one's mental state, self-doubt, and putting pressure on oneself.

But, as Pelé himself indicates, "confidence" and "calmness" seem inadequate descriptions of what he felt. They fail to convey the depth and intensity of a feeling of power verging on the mystical, a kind of spiritual power.

The great Russian weight lifter Yuri Vlasov speaks in a similar vein in describing "the precious, white moment" of athletic excellence.

> At the peak of tremendous and victorious effort, while the blood is pounding in your head, all suddenly becomes quiet within you. Everything seems clearer and whiter than ever before, as if great spotlights had been turned on. At that moment you have the conviction that you contain all the power in the world, that you are capable of everything, that you have wings. There is no more precious moment in life than this, the white moment, and you will work very hard for years just to taste it again.

In his self-titled autobiography, *Sadaharu Oh: A Zen Way of Baseball*, Japanese baseball's greatest slugger describes the experience of heightened mastery and power in explicitly spiritual terms. This may be because he approached batting as an endeavor of the spirit. In 1962, after a disappointing start to his career, Oh began training with Hiroshi Arakawa, who incorporated into his instruction principles from Japan's martial ways. Oh learned to center mind and body in his *hara*, the focal point of spirit/energy located about two fingers below the navel. As his training progressed, Oh was able to direct that energy out through his bat, to wait in concentration for the exact moment to strike at the ball, to read the motion and even the intent of opposing pitchers, and much more. His game caught fire, and by the end of the 1964 season he had already won three of his eventual fifteen home-run titles: "The home runs rocketed off my bat almost as though a power beyond my own was responsible." He was, so to speak, in the Oh zone: "I went to the plate with no thought other than this moment of hitting confronting me. It was everything. And in the midst of it, in the midst of chanting and cheering crowds, colors, noises, hot and cold weather, the glare of lights, or rain on my skin, there was only this noiseless, colorless, heatless void in which the pitcher and I together enacted our certain preordained ritual of the home run."

Athletes commonly describe perceptual enhancement as an aspect of the zone. For Michael Jordan, "The rim seems like a big ol' huge bucket." According to the New York Knicks' John Starks, "It's like you see something just before it really happens." John Olerud of the Toronto Blue Jays says, "When things are going well, there seems to be more time to react to a pitch. And it doesn't matter what that pitch is. It's just that it feels like you have more time to react."

The experience Olerud describes is known among psychologists as *elongated time*, seeing fast-moving events in slow motion. For a few athletes at the very pinnacle of their sport, it occurs so frequently that it seems perfectly natural. Such an athlete was the basketball great Jerry West. Inarguably, West was one of the greatest ever to play the game, and for the past decade and a half he has been the sport's finest general manager. But like many of the best athletes, West was merely average as a coach, particularly because of his notorious impatience with his players. After his Los Angeles Lakers lost to the Portland Trailblazers in the 1976 playoffs, West expressed his disappointment to Blazers center Bill Walton: "Many of the players rationalize their mistakes by claiming everything is happening so fast on the court that they get mixed up . . . but when I played, everything seemed to be happening in slow motion out there. I could see what was happening in advance, and anticipate plays." As anyone who saw him play knows, West was unsurpassed at using his talents to the fullest. But he was also exceptionally gifted, and it seems that he found it difficult to coach those less blessed than he.

As we've seen, experiences in the zone vary in depth and in the qualities to which they give rise. At the most profound level, one glimpses, in the words of Bart Giamatti, "a moment when we are all free of all constraint of all kinds, when pure energy and pure order create an instant of complete coherence." The rower Michael Filippone says, "It's like a higher level, being perfectly in the moment, a phenomenal feeling, a spiritual feeling. It becomes effortless to work hard. That's the most precious thing in the sport." His brother David concurs: "It's a mystical feeling, with the eight hearts of the crew beating as one." In these ecstatic moments, something altogether transcendent pierces the cloud of life's confusion to illuminate an underlying perfection.

Whatever the degree of intensity, athletes strive to recreate and sustain the experience of the zone. According to Rick Wolff, the often bizarre pregame rituals of athletes are, at least in part, a means of mental preparation, a way "to seduce your brain into getting into the flow." The examples are countless. Before each home game, the former Stanford basketball star Val Whiting would have a friend stand in the exact same spot in front of her dorm and wish her good luck. Ty Cobb said that to preserve a hitting streak, "I always go to the ballpark by the same route, put on my uniform the same way. I try to recall which sock I'd donned first. If it was my left I will not give the right one precedence for a raise in pay."

Meggyesy agrees with Wolff. Sports fans, writers, even athletes themselves may regard these rituals as mere superstition, but they serve a practical function. Before a game, Meggyesy would tie and untie his shoelaces twenty or more times. "If you had asked me why, I'd have said it just didn't feel right. But this sort of ritual activity is part of the process of mental preparation. It helps induce a state of consciousness." It might also have been a good way of "binding" the anxiety of pregame jitters.

Rituals may help, but clearly they are only a piece of the puzzle. The big question remains: How do you get into the zone? "If I knew that," says Wolff, "I'd be a millionaire many times over." Coaches, athletes, and owners would all love to bottle the zone. And they will shell out the big bucks for its formula. And as a trip to the bookstore will show, more than a few have done quite well for themselves claiming to have it. But sports psychologists are divided on the question of whether it even makes sense to try to get there.

In his *Times* magazine piece on the zone, Larry Shainberg discusses the work of Keith Henschen, an applied sports psychologist at the University of Utah, in Salt Lake City. As Shainberg writes, for Henschen, "the zone is a practical matter." Henschen's program draws upon techniques from meditation, the martial arts, and psychotherapy, along with conventional methods of athletic training. Henschen says, "No one can reach such levels by snapping their fingers, but the purpose of the exercises I use is to help an athlete get to the zone more frequently."

But some sports psychologists, such as Bob Rotella, disagree with Henschen's premise that the zone experience can be intentionally cultivated. Rotella, who specializes in working with golfers, says, "It happens when it happens," and thinking about it just gets in the way of it happening at all. And he's got a point. Self-transcendence, a characteristic of the zone at its most profound, cannot be produced by force of will. As any meditator, musician, or martial artist can tell you, when the self *tries* to go beyond itself, it just creates more . . . well, more self. No bootstrap principle applies.

To Forget the Self

Mastery of one's craft and relaxed concentration are necessary, but they are not sufficient. Visualization, meditation, counseling, progressive relaxation, and the other techniques of sports psychology can enhance one's physical and mental abilities, but they cannot produce self-transcendence. For if there is one defining characteristic of that moment of pure intuition, a *sine qua non*, it is that it is effortless and unpredictable, a kind of state of grace.

This is, after all, the paradox of inspiration, no matter what the field. You must work and work and work some more, but the golden moment cannot be produced through an act of will. You can only prepare the ground for it to happen. As one Zen master has said, "Enlightenment is an accident, but some activities make you accident prone."

The reference here to Zen is fitting, because in Zen practice one engages this paradox directly. One is exhorted to practice rigorously, pursuing enlightenment with a sense of urgency, as if one were "extinguishing a fire upon your head," as a traditional saying has it. And yet, as Maezumi Rōshi writes, "When you seek after enlightenment, enlightenment will elude you. Yet without seeking after it, you will never realize it." This can be a real problem.

In a famous passage from Genjōkōan (Actualizing the Fundamental Point), Zen master Dōgen writes:

> To study the buddha way is to study the self.
> To study the self is to forget the self.

The object of one's seeking, the buddha way, is not apart from oneself, and the way to realize this experientially is by forgetting the self. But how does one forget the self? Certainly not by trying. That would be like trying not to think of a white elephant: the more you try, the more insistent the thought becomes. One forgets the self by becoming one with the task at hand. *Zazen*, or seated meditation, is the quintessential form for this focused awareness, but it can be practiced anywhere and anytime. As practice deepens and matures, one may have a sudden intuitive glimpse of the intrinsic unity of all things. In Zen this experience is called *kenshō* or *satori*, and it is the subject of Dōgen's next line:

> To forget the self is to be enlightened by all things.

Zen tradition can, I believe, shed some light on some of the contradicting views about the zone and also on what is perhaps the most significant difference between flow and peak experience. This is not to say that peak experience, flow, or the zone are satori by some other name. They are not. There may be some interesting correspondences and qualities that overlap, but to explore them adequately would require the kind of thorough study that is the stuff of doctoral dissertations and without which you get only superficial comparisons. But a Zen perspective on the relationship between practice and enlightenment may help clarify structural issues in the relationship between self-effort and self-transcendence in sport.

Some of those we have heard from believe there are things you can do to get into the zone. Others say it happens when it happens, and you're better off not thinking about it. Parallel to this, Csikszentmihalyi regards flow as an experience that one can bring about through one's own effort. When certain conditions are met, flow will occur. For Maslow, peak experiences are spontaneous epiphanies, in which there is no link between one's actions and the experience. Indeed, Maslow once said that he himself had never had a peak experience. Jackson's study showed a close relationship between flow, peak experience, and peak performance. While the relationship between flow and peak performance was quite clear, the connection between flow and peak experience was not. To help clarify the situation, Jackson suggests that flow be regarded as a process and peak performance and experience be seen as outcomes. It makes sense, but if we stick to Maslow's definition, the connection between process and outcome is much more certain in the case of peaks in performance than in experience. For, as we can see in experiences like those of Russell and Pelé, certain moments are discontinuous with the preparation leading up to them. Like the relationship in Zen between practice and satori, certain experiences of athletes represent a qualitative leap in consciousness.

These transcendent moments in sport are not produced by effort, yet without years of diligent effort, they don't happen. So the question becomes, how does one prepare the ground? What kind of effort leads beyond self-conscious effort? The answer is subtle, at least to the ego, whose habit is to go directly after what it wants. That approach might work for a lot of things, but it won't work in this case. It is, I think, a matter of readiness. Unpredictably, the moment of grace breaks upon you, and the question is whether you are ready to receive it. That moment cannot be cultivated, but the state of readiness can be.

One component of this readiness is craftsmanship. Ravizza found that mastery of the basic skills of one's sport is an important precondition for the peak experience. Rather than skill, I like to think of this component as craftsmanship, a broader term that includes skill but also suggests a certain attitude that elevates skill beyond the level of self-concern.

According to Csikszentmihalyi, flow happens "when a person's body or mind is stretched to its limits" in pursuit of a worthwhile goal. What makes that stretching possible is the development of skills adequate to the challenge of the task. Whatever the level of one's ability, there must be a balance between the demands of the activity and one's ability to meet those demands. If the activity is too easy, boredom will result; if it is too hard, it will cause anxiety.

But this balance is not static. With greater skill comes a greater ability to channel one's energy into the task at hand and to respond fully to increasingly complex demands for action. Regardless of one's level of expertise, without a disciplined cultivation of skill, one's potential, and the potential of the game, will go unfulfilled.

Skill is about realizing the goals of the self. Craftsmanship is about that, too, but not only that. It is also about realizing the intrinsic nature of the game: its formal dynamics and inherent satisfactions, the gifts bestowed and the demands made on those who play it. It entails appreciation of subtlety, nuance, and detail; it includes care for the game's meaning, history, and culture. As in art, dedication to the craft of a sport elicits a purity of intention, because one's point of reference is more the game than it is the self.

In his famous essay on Ted Williams's last game, "Hub Fans Bid Kid Adieu," John Updike distills into a single sentence the essence of craftsmanship in sport by describing a man who was one of its finest embodiments. "For me, Williams is the classic ballplayer of the game on a hot August weekday before a small crowd, when the only thing at stake is the tissue-thin difference between a thing done well and a thing done ill."

In *Sports in the Western World*, William J. Baker tells an anecdote about another Red Sox great, Carl Yastrzemski, that clues us into a second component of readiness for the moment of athletic grace. As Yastrzemski was nearing both his fortieth birthday and his three-thousandth base hit, he was asked about the source of his endurance. "What's your secret, Yaz? What keeps you going after all these years?" It was, finally, not money, fame, or team loyalty; it was "the competition. Facing the pitcher one on one. Once you get into the batter's box, pride takes over. Nobody can help. Something inside keeps me going." For Baker, the "something inside" of which Yastrzemski speaks is a "competitive impulse that is as old as the human race."

Pride in oneself, love of competition—these are, of course, clichés of sports culture. That they are essential attributes of accomplished athletes is beyond dispute. But just as skill is contained within the broader idea of craftsmanship, so is the competitive spirit part of something larger, something, again, not based in self-concern.

Bill Russell, the consummate competitor, pointed to this larger idea when he described those peaks of magic when "the game would be in a white heat of competition, yet somehow I wouldn't feel competitive." In such moments, competition is transformed, as one's opponent becomes one's partner in lifting the level of play. Here the competitive spirit finds its true ground.

The German philosopher Hans-Georg Gadamer writes of that "deep play" in which the individual ceases to stand apart from the full field of action. The game seems to have a life of its own, and one senses oneself as part of a larger design. The individual player is encompassed within, and is an expression of, the game's intrinsic patterns. The game plays the player. The competitive impulse is grounded in the irresistible desire to achieve that perfection that reveals the game's inherent form.

Paul Weiss writes that "athletes are excellence in the guise of men." (And, of course, women too—he wrote this in 1969. It is worth noting, however, that this is but an innocent example of the strong sexist bias that mars Weiss's otherwise fine book. One must hope, even assume, that, were the book written more recently, time would have ameliorated this attitude.) "Competitive spirit" seems too paltry a term to describe this passion for excellence, which goes far beyond the ego's will to succeed. More accurately, it is a sense of devotion that drives an athlete toward the realization of the game's perfect form, something that can't be grasped, only glimpsed.

It is said that God is in the details. Nowhere is this more evident than in sport. To mean anything, the lofty devotion to excellence must be translated into a practical passion for detail. In his portrait of Bill Bradley's brilliant basketball career at Princeton, *A Sense of Where You Are*, John McPhee captures this passion that all top athletes share and for which Bradley was famous:

> "There are five parts to the hook shot," [Bradley] explains to anyone who asks. As he continues, he picks up a ball and stands about eighteen feet from a basket. "Crouch," he says, crouching, and goes on to demonstrate the other moves. "Turn your head to look for the basket, step, kick, follow through with your arms." Once as he was explaining this to me, the ball curled around the rim and failed to go in.
>
> "What happened then?" I asked him.
> "I didn't kick high enough." he said.
> "Do you always know exactly why you've missed a shot?
> "Yes," he said, missing another one.
> "What happened that time?"
> "I was talking to you. I didn't concentrate. The secret of shooting is concentration."

To play with inspiration, one must give oneself over to one's game. It is no different for athletes than it is for artists. I am reminded of a story about a famous writer who was approached by an eager undergraduate wanting to know the Secret of being a writer herself. After a few moments' thought, the old pro answered, "Well, do you love words?"

Just as words are the basic stuff of a writer's craft, so are the body's rehearsed and ritualized movements the stuff of the athlete's craft. Appreciating and taking delight in the ordering of mind and body that the game imposes brings one fully into the activity. The freedom a sport bestows is a product of the discipline it demands. To play it right, you've got to love the game.

Only when these two conditions—craftsmanship and devotion—are met can a third one be met as well: immersion in the activity. An archer who is worried about missing the target will miss it. A batter who is focused on whether he will steal second will not make it to first. The name of the game is to set the busy-ness of the mind aside and fully bring one's attention to bear on the immediate task at hand. According to the professional archer Tim Strickland, "Your conscious mind always wants to help you, but usually it messes you up. But you can't just set it aside. You've got to get it involved. The thing you have to do is anchor it in technique. Then your unconscious mind, working with your motor memory, will take over the shooting for you."

Athletes will often describe this as playing by instinct. In fact, nothing could be further from the truth. Instinct refers to behaviors that are genetically programmed, and the accomplishment of a difficult athletic feat is anything but that. Such accomplishment is a highly complex integration of sophisticated skills, perceptions, and knowledge.

In *Men at Work: The Craft of Baseball*—one of the finest books ever written on the game and an important resource for this book—George Will thoroughly demolishes the simplistic notion that excellence in the game is based on instinct or natural talent. He recounts being told by then–Oakland A's manager Tony La Russa, one of the game's finest strategists, that what are called instincts are in fact the consequence of "an accumulation of baseball information. They [instincts] are uses of that information as the basis of decision-making as game situations develop. Your instincts may say 'pitch out now' and later you may say, 'Why did I do that?' When you trust your gut you are trusting a lot of stuff that is there from the past."

A pitcher may say, "I was just trying to throw strikes," or a batter may claim he was "just looking for a good ball to hit," but as Will shows, this apparent simplicity is quite at odds with the real complexities of processing tremendous amounts of information about the game's crucial variables. But unless they are prompted to discuss the nuances of the sport—something that few journalists show the patience for—players and coaches retreat into a recitation of the familiar clichés.

Although an accomplished performance is anything but instinctual, the idea crops up too frequently to deny that there is something about it that makes it feel that way. That something is immersion. What feels like instinct is the absence of the fear, doubt, worry, and unnecessary deliberation that result from self-consciousness. But whereas instinct is a regression to a level of functioning prior to the formation of self-consciousness, what we see in sport is a highly refined mode of intuitive functioning that transcends self-consciousness. It is a harmonization of the faculties of body and mind, each doing the task that is appropriate to it, and a full trust in the knowledge that years of work have made second nature. There is, in Zen terms, "nothing extra"—no ego standing apart from the action encumbering it with useless commentary. Or as an Italian proverb has it, "Learn how to do it, then forget you know how."

Michael Novak describes this experience beautifully, though he too, unfortunately, speaks of instinct where what is meant is intuition:

> This is one of the great inner secrets of sports. There is a certain point of unity within the self, and between the self and its world, a

certain complicity and magnetic mating, a certain harmony that conscious mind and will cannot direct. Perhaps analysis and the separate mastery of each element are required before the instincts are ready to assume command, but only at first. Command by instinct is swifter, subtler, deeper, more accurate, more in touch with reality than command by conscious mind.

It is, of course, not really that well kept a secret. Almost anyone who has worked hard in some field of play can recall a moment of astonishment when all of it—body, mind, and the skill that runs through both—came together and the boundaries of possibility seemed to open wide before one's eyes. In these moments, everything you do seems to turn to gold. I still savor a few such long-ago moments—on a basketball court, a soccer field, a ski slope—with the same vivid detail as I recall my first kiss.

One does not have to be a player to sense this. As Shainberg observes, "Our fascination with the zone, and indeed with sport in general, may be due, in part at least, to the possibilities it reveals, the energy and strength and flexibility of the organism when liberated from its ordinary neurological and psychological constraints." As spectators, we are drawn irresistibly by the thrill of witnessing the drama of self-surpassing play. In this way, athletics awaken and invite us to our own exceptional possibilities.

Novak writes that the discovery of this "secret" harmony "take's one's breath away." This is another instance of the link between athletics and aesthetics. A moment of athletic beauty displays the self finding full accord in the wholeness of its situation. It shows existence aglow in all its rightness. Metaphorically, we recognize in the actions of another that way of being to which our own deepest inclination always points us.

Earlier in this century, D. T. Suzuki nearly single-handedly introduced Zen Buddhism to the West. At the center of Dr. Suzuki's discussion was the experience of satori; it was for him the key reference point for understanding the entirety of Zen thought and practice. As the religious scholar Huston Smith has pointed out, fascination with the sudden, dramatic breakthrough that is satori was to a large degree what made Suzuki's writings so compelling.

In the thirty years since Dr. Suzuki's death at the age of ninety-six, Zen has sunk its roots deep into Western soil, and its teachings have been taken up by many tens of thousands. Over the years, Suzuki has often been criticized for so emphasizing satori. The reasons are many: focusing on satori presents a distorted and incomplete picture of Zen; it draws attention away from Zen's other, less exciting aspects, which are the stuff of a life of practice; it encourages dilettantism at the expense of ripening discipline. Perhaps most significantly, focusing on satori hinders practice by establishing for the ego a goal to be attained in the future, something quite at odds with the practice of forgetting the self in full concentration in the present.

Such criticisms are valid, but they are also unfair. Dr. Suzuki was introducing Zen to an audience that knew little, if anything, about it. Because it is so discontinuous with everyday experience, Suzuki's descriptions of the extraordinariness of satori served to open wide the minds of Western readers to the possibilities of practice. Satori is not the last word in Zen, but it is a good start to a long conversation.

I tell this story because the place of satori in Zen is analogous to the place of the zone in understanding the secret life of sport. Because of their power, because of what they show about human possibilities, because they are so compelling, it is tempting to conclude that transcendent moments are definitive of sport's spiritual dimensions. They are not. But in such moments the potent reality of the secret life is made most evident and its key themes are brought into sharp relief. As with satori and Zen, the zone does not exhaust our understanding of the secret life of sport. It is not an end point. It is a point from which we depart with a deeper and richer sense of the inner landscape through which we travel.

CHAPTER THREE

The Second World

There we would stand,
within the gap left between world and toy,
upon a spot which, from the first beginning,
had been established for a pure event.

RAINER MARIA RILKE

Michael Roberts opens his entertaining and insightful book *Fans: How We Go Crazy over Sports* by telling of an old two-paragraph article he once found tucked into the sports pages of the daily paper. In October 1973 a Colorado man had attempted suicide by shooting himself in the head. Earlier that day, the Denver Broncos had fumbled seven times while losing to the Chicago Bears. The man left a note referring to the game, reading, "I have been a Broncos fan since the Broncos were first organized, and I can't stand their fumbling anymore."

The man survived the attempt. As Roberts tells us, "Poor marksmanship was all that averted a human sacrifice to the football gods; maybe they were appeased by the gesture itself." The incident stuck in Roberts's mind, and over time he grew "ever more intrigued with the hold spectator sports and jock-heroes have on their followers."

It seems ironic that *Fans* and the present book have such similar starting points, in view of the vast, often opposing, differences in what Roberts and I have to say. Roberts writes with the mordant wit of a sports cynic, for whom our society's sports obsession is something corrupt and unwholesome. Sport is, for Roberts, a "source of shameless propaganda," a "subject of nonsense beliefs" and an "instrument of disreputable purposes." The suicide attempt of that unfortunate Broncos fan is but one example of our sports sickness.

My differences with Roberts are less on matters of fact than on the interpretation of those facts. Most of our differences stem from a single one, that of perspective. One perspective is that of an insider attempting to make intelligible his devotion; the other is that of an outsider for whom such devotion speaks of the deluded and misplaced energies of others. For the outsider, the diagnostic problem is to find the individual and social failings that cause our sports pathology. For the insider, it is a matter of finding what C. J. Jung spoke of as the gods in the disease.

In relating the "fumbles" story to friends, I found that their reactions mirrored this contrast of insider and outsider. Those who are not sports fans smiled ruefully or sadly shook their heads. The sports fans, on the other hand, all broke into laughter. When I stopped to think about the difference in the responses, I found I could more easily understand why the nonfans responded as they did than why I and the other fans thought the incident so funny. Why would we laugh at such a sad and pathetic gesture?

Freud saw that laughter betokens recognition. Think of how great comedians—Chaplin, Keaton, Lenny Bruce, Richard Pryor, Woody Allen—wring humor from miseries, large and small. I think recognition was at work in our seemingly callous response—it was a kind of gallows humor. Anyone who has given himself or herself over to love of a sport knows that that love must be suffered as well as enjoyed. Though it is rare (fortunately) that a fan's emotional attachment is carried to such extremes, we are all familiar with the power of sport to bedazzle and overwhelm reason. We have all, in one way or another, taken at least a peek over the precipice into which that poor fellow jumped: we secretly rejoice at an injury to the opposing team's star player; we lust for violent revenge for a perceived wrong done to our side; we become mean or neglectful while under the influence of fan frenzy; we despair that the loss of a favorite team is indicative of a personal flaw or proof of a cosmic one. (Apropos of this, on the day of this writing, I saw in *Sports Illustrated* mention of a "Chiefs Grief" therapy group to help Kansas City football fans get over their team's recent playoff loss to the Indianapolis Colts. It ran under the heading "This Week's Sign That the Apocalypse Is upon Us.") This is all to say that we lose our day-to-day bearings in the emotional sweep of the game. Like the influx of a godly energy, the second world of sport exerts a possessive effect, an effect that can enrich the soul or engulf the self. And the line between the two is often unclear.

Like many a baseball team owner to follow, the beer baron Christian Frederick Wilhelm Van der Ahe, owner of a professional Saint Louis club in the late nineteenth century, was a pompous boor. He indulged his grandiose ego through such means as making his players march behind him single file at railroad stations, as well as other such Steinbrenian displays. Nevertheless, he deserves credit for two great contributions to American sports. He was the first to sell hot dogs at the ballpark, and in referring to his team's followers as "fanatics" in his thickly accented English, he originated the word *fan*.

According to my dictionary, a fan is an "enthusiastic devotee," while a fanatic is one whose enthusiasm is "excessive" and "uncritical." But the Latin root of the words reveals a deeper layer of meaning. *Fanatic* derives from the Latin *fanaticus*, "belonging to the temple of the god of that place; being inspired by the local divinity." We can then say, with at least etymological justification, that to be a fan is to be inspired and to deepen one's connection to a particular place through the agency of a power beyond the self.

Following the trail of these words and their associations is instructive. In the ancient world the inspiration of a divine power was something to be highly prized. Though traces of this sensibility persist—as when artists speak of being seized by a muse—it has for the most part retreated into the psychic underground. Beginning with the Greek philosophers, Western consciousness has increasingly turned toward reason, rather than feeling, as its primary mode of apprehending the world and toward the rational discernment of laws, rather than the imaginative exposition of myths, as the means of interpreting that world. In the process, the capacity to experience the influx of transpersonal energies came to be distrusted, and the mythological personification of those energies, the gods, were held to be malevolent or unreal. Rather than being seen as a bridge to the sacred, divine inspiration was reduced to irrational frenzy or mere foolishness. But in the word *fan* something affirmative is restored to our devoted enthusiasms, and a link is formed with the mythologically informed past. That sport should be the vehicle for this is not coincidental, for sport has maintained that link more strongly than perhaps any other contemporary institution.

Between Jest and Earnest

The link between sport and myth is most readily apparent in sport's rhetorical style. When Roberts writes of a fan's failed suicide as an unsuccessful "human sacrifice to the football gods," he is, of course, mocking the passion fans invest in sport and the value they ascribe to them. But even Roberts, sports cynic that he is, resorts to mythic language to convey the potency of the feelings he addresses.

Mythic language insists itself upon sport. The realm of sport requires a mode of expression adequate to its intensity. Sport needs dramatic language that brings to light the perennial themes it enacts. It needs extravagant language that evokes awareness of the sublime and frightening dimensions of human experience it displays. It needs humorous language that deflates its pretensions, mirrors its absurdities, and delights in its ridiculousness. The method of sport is play, and so sport requires that its mode of discourse be playful. Like myth.

In his classic study of humankind's myths, *The Masks of God*, Joseph Campbell writes, "In all the wild imaginings of mythology a fanciful spirit is playing on the border-line between jest and earnest." In his choice of words, Campbell is acknowledging his debt to the thought of the Dutch cultural historian Johan Huizinga, who in his pioneering study of play's essential role in culture, *Homo Ludens* (Man the Player), refers to play as a borderline realm, "between jest and earnest," standing apart from ordinary life.

Campbell sees a structural link between play and myth, both operating according to the same internal logic, the logic of "as if." Both myth and play are make-believe. A world separate from the demands and constraints of ordinary life is imagined, and by entering that world *as if* it were true, one is absorbed into its meaning structure. Within that second world, experience is given coherence, shape, vitality, and value. By establishing an "as if" realm of order and significance, both myth and play serve as models by which consciousness can perceive those same attributes in the self, society, and the cosmos.

In *The Power of Myth* Campbell observes, "A key difference between mythology and our Judeo-Christian religion is that the imagery of mythology is rendered with humor. You realize that the image is symbolic of something. You're at a distance from it." Like myth, sport calls for humor in its exposition. It needs the distance humor provides in order to preserve the integrity of its reality, to shield itself from the functional claims of practical life.

Sadly, this sensibility is all too often absent in today's sports culture. The purveyors of sport are adept at massaging and manipulating the public's genuine longing for the mythic resonance their product provides. But the packaged platitudes and ponderous melodramatics they present is self-conscious mythmaking, and hence not mythmaking at all. The heedless encroachment of commercial (or, for that matter, ideological) interests on the second world—the make-believe, "as if" world—blurs the boundary that sustains its reality.

The boundary of sport needs a proper balance of jest and earnest. Admittedly, the balance is difficult to maintain. Sport cannot escape its social context, nor should it try to. Sport is not about purity. It thrives on the unreasonable attachments it triggers. It is energized by the uneasy tensions that continually crop up at its boundaries, where passions pass forward and back between the second world and the world of everyday experience. The boundary that sets the worlds apart is also the place where realities meet. Confusion at the boundary of the borderline realm that exists between jest and earnest is one of the means by which sport instructs us in containing and channeling the free energies it excites. To form a proper relationship with the second world, one must continually find that boundary.

The difficulty of maintaining balance is further enhanced by the inflation that is so much a part of sport's rhetorical style. Sport needs language that conveys its possessive power. It needs hyperbole, but it also needs irony. Irony is the necessary corrective to sport's tendency toward cloying seriousness and pretension. Irony creates distance from the seductive quagmire of misconstrued symbols and metaphors. As one coach wisely put it, football players may take the field with shouts of "This is war," but marines don't take a beach crying, "This is football."

One of the most memorable passages in sports journalism is Red Smith's masterful telling of what was perhaps baseball's most dramatic moment. On October 3, 1951, the New York Giants' Bobby Thomson homered against the archrival Brooklyn Dodgers, thus bringing to victorious conclusion the Giants' extraordinary come-from-behind bid for the National League pennant. For the Giants and their fans, "the Shot Heard 'Round the World" brought an eruption of joyous delirium; for Dodgers players and fans, it was a crushing heartbreak. Writing for the *New York Herald Tribune*, Smith captured the immensity of feeling ignited by "the Miracle at Coogan's Bluff": "Now it is done, now the story ends. And there is no way to tell of it. The art of fiction is dead. Reality has strangled invention. Only the utterly impossible, the inexpressibly fantastic, can ever be plausible again."

Smith's words are, of course, preposterous if taken literally. The truth they convey is a poetic one, an immediate evocation of an experience too large for the confines of literal description. The language makes fantastic claims, not realistic ones. The words are not, however, delivered with tongue in cheek, but rather with the wink of an eye. He knows we know it is not *really* true, and we know he knows we know it.

Overwrought extravagance of language is another link between myth and sport. The archetypal psychologist James Hillman writes, "Mythical talk must be full of hyperbole; the gods live in the highs and lows." The secret life of sport leads through the same terrain. One-time Boston Red Sox shortstop Johnny Pesky described it thus: "Baseball can build you up to the sky one day and the next day you have to climb a stepladder to look up to a snake." (And Pesky should know, having perpetrated the heartbreaking play in the 1946 World Series, between Saint Louis and Boston, in which he held the ball as the Cardinals' Enos Slaughter scored the series' winning run from first base on Harry Walker's outfield single.)

Bill Russell calls sport a "land of exaggeration . . . where no rigid truth has to be respected." The more outrageous the claim, the better, and the sky is the limit. Just as Campbell sees humor underlying mythology, so does Russell see humor in sport. In both cases, rhetorical excess and humor go hand in hand, bringing to each a kind of humility. Unburdened of ideological seriousness and modest in their claims on truth, sport and myth delight in the free play of language. Russell points to athletes' nicknames as exemplary of this predilection. Think of Earl the Pearl, Clyde the Glide, and Hakeem the Dream; Sweetness Payton and Hacksaw Reynolds; Tiny Archibald and Big Daddy Lipscomb; Dizzy Dean and his brother Daffy; the Gashouse Gang, the Fearsome Foursome, Murderers' Row; George Herman "Babe" "the Bambino" "the Sultan of Swat" "the King of Clout" "the Monarch of Mayhem" Ruth. And, of course, the Greatest, Muhammad Ali, who is not only the greatest ever to have stepped into the ring but is also the all-time master of sports talk. A memorable example of his rhetorical skill is this self-reflective observation (which I've rendered into verse, as its merits demand) made before his amazing victory over the seemingly invincible George Foreman:

> Only last week
> I murdered a rock,
> Injured stone,
> Hospitalized a brick.
> I'm so mean
> I make medicine sick.

The language of sport is one of the few refuges of mythic consciousness in our culture's mainstream. It is where we can speak of things mythic—of heroes and their trials, of Fate and Immortality, of wondrous deeds—from that essential borderline perspective between jest and earnest. Like myth—and unlike religious and secular doctrines of progress—sports talk turns imaginatively to the past: to records, legends, dynasties, and golden ages, to ancient emotions and tribal symbols, to paradisal remembrance and childhood experience. It is inevitably metaphoric and symbolic and is, therefore, necessarily concerned with our deepest yearnings and imaginings. It provides us with imagery for describing the events of our lives and with dramatic structures through which these events gather meaning, richness, and depth. The language of sport is a lens through which we view ourselves and our experience.

Michael Novak observes that "we are inexpert in the realm of myth," and so we are unprepared to understand sport. Despite our abundant enthusiasm, our view of sport is impoverished by a lack of ideas equal to the subject. Unfortunately, having pointed this out, Novak does little to clarify just *how* mythic thinking illuminates sport.

The Gods Will Be Present

In order to better understand the interplay of sport and myth, I turned to the ideas of Carl Jung. Although earlier thinkers, especially Nietzsche, recognized that myth was not only a carrier of ideas but also a mode of consciousness, it was Jung, more than anyone else, who developed a framework through which modern consciousness could make a living, existential connection to the mythic world. In his work as a psychiatrist, Jung found that the recurrent symbols, images, and stories of world mythology appeared regularly and apparently spontaneously in the dreams and fantasies of his patients. Long and repeated observation of this phenomenon led him to reason that these representations arose from "definitive motifs" innate to the human psyche, the contents of a collective unconscious that is the underlying stratum of all psychic life.

Jung conceived these primordial images, or *archetypes*, as he eventually came to call them, as deep structures that shape and direct experience—our behaviors, attitudes, perceptions, ideas, fantasies—along definite lines. Archetypes, like instincts, are potentialities, and like instincts, they are not apprehended directly. We know the archetypes through symbolic forms that manifest their specific energies. These representations— goddesses and gods, religious imagery, mythic narratives—are bearers of sacred significance, of meaning, power, and irreducible value.

The predicament of modern consciousness, as Jung saw it, is that Western civilization, over the centuries, has relied increasingly on the powers of the rational mind to define and mediate experience. In the process we have freed ourselves from irrational beliefs—or so we like to think. But we have made the mistake of supposing that all that is nonrational is irrational, and in so doing we have split off consciousness from the deeper strata of the psyche. Our capacity to respond to the symbols through which the primal energies speak has withered, and with that we have lost the sense of vitality that comes from symbolic contact with the natural phenomena of the psyche and the world. As Jung observed, "We have stripped all things of their mystery and numinosity; nothing is holy any longer."

Throughout human history, religions have provided symbols and myths that connect consciousness with the deep forces in the psyche. But as Jung saw it, conventional religion, at least in the West, had grown anemic, its rituals, stories, and symbols drained of numinous content. Cut off from nature and instinct, focused on stale doctrine, religion had ceased to be an adequate link to the experience of the sacred.

Jung saw modernity as the setting of a great spiritual drama, in which what is at stake is humankind's soul. The great accomplishments and benefits of the rational tradition have come at a high price. We moderns pride ourselves on our success at cleansing the world of primitive symbols and beliefs. But while we may ignore the gods, they do not ignore us. Forced from our world, the numina have retreated underground to the unconscious.

For all our sophistication, we are for the most part childishly maladapted in our relationship to the primal powers in which our lives are rooted. We may ignore our mythic needs, but we remain mythic creatures. We may ignore the symbolic forms—the "message carriers"—that connect the conscious mind with its unconscious depths, but we remain subject to their power. Although our culture provides little in the way of graspable forms—myths, images, rituals—that would promote a conscious relationship between the ego and the deeper layers of the psyche, we still crave these forms and that relationship with a hunger as true and as powerful as any instinct.

Jung was fond of quoting the old Latin saying: "Whether invited or not, the gods will be present." Today, lacking adequate containers that would provide the recognition they are due, the gods come to us anyway, distorted by repression, pathologized and unbidden, overwhelming consciousness with fixations, dark moods, fears, obsessions. Lacking a developed mythic consciousness that would allow us to approach the numina imaginatively and integrate them into a coherent psychic pattern, we are forced to live them out unconsciously. Zeus presides over us in the person of opportunistic demagogues. Venus stares out from magazine covers through the starving eyes of supermodels. We look to political or religious ideologies to provide the unifying vision of the great mythic narratives. Friends, lovers, and public figures continually disappoint because they are human beings and not the symbolic figures we unconsciously ask them to be. With passion and conviction in their literal significance, we project archetypal fantasies into the world and onto ourselves. And then, more often than not, we find that we can't stand the fumbles.

Given the great psychological importance Jungians ascribe to the mythology of ancient Greece, and given the mythic significance the Greeks assigned to sport, I had expected to find considerable commentary on the relationship between sport and myth in the Jungian literature. I was mistaken. Several weeks of hunting around yielded precious little on the topic, though what little I did find suggested the presence of a rich vein waiting to be tapped.

For help, I called a friend connected with the Jung Institute in

San Francisco. Though the subject was of zero interest to my friend, he was able to refer me to an analyst at the institute who he thought would be of help. As it turned out, he was right.

Mana

Tom Singer is an experienced Jungian analyst and an avid sports fan who takes obvious delight in talking about the territory where these two pursuits meet. His love for the topic was evident in our first conversation, and it never waned. Indeed, following a meeting or phone call, I'd often find a lengthy message on my answering machine expanding upon a point we had discussed earlier, suggesting a resource he had just remembered, or providing the citation for a passage he had quoted.

In our initial phone conversation, I described how I had come to call him. Agreeing that the mythic significance of sport was a conspicuously neglected topic in Jungian literature, he said, "As to why that is, I can only guess. Jung's main psychological focus was on the individuation process, which he saw as a concern of middle age. He probably relegated athletics to the area of *puer*, or youthful, psychology. Since then, most Jungians have probably just followed the precedent he set."

He paused for a few seconds, then something else sparked his thinking. "On the other hand, Jungians tend, by and large, to be pretty removed from popular culture. They're not accustomed to applying their ideas to something as much in the mainstream as sports. For the most part, we're a pretty nerdy group." In down-to-earth language, this echoed Paul Weiss's observation about intellectuals' neglect of sport. I looked forward to talking further with this guy.

We made a date to get together a couple of weeks later. Before hanging up, he recommended that I try to get hold of a recent anthology of writings by Jungians called *Psyche and Sports*. It took a bit of hunting around, but I soon tracked down a copy, and fortunately so, since several of the essays have proven most helpful. Though he did not mention it, one of the chapters is by Singer himself, a condensed version of the book *A Fan's Guide to Baseball Fever*, which he co-wrote with Stuart Copens, also a psychiatrist, and the cartoonist Mitchell Rose.

Baseball Fever is a delight. Subtitled *The Official Medical Reference*, it looks humorously at the peculiar effects the game elicits in its devoted followers as symptoms of a psychiatric disorder. Parodying the language and format of diagnostic manuals, *Baseball Fever* covers such aspects of the disorder as etiology, statistical data, and symptomatic behavior (mood swings, masochistic tendencies, intellectual defenses, homicidal impulses, and so forth). Although it was written to entertain, in poking fun at the excesses to which love of the game may lead, the book makes some serious points. For all its good-naturedness, it reminds us of the gods at work in this particularly benign disease.

For our first meeting, I crossed the bay from my home in Oakland to Tom's office in a three-story Victorian in San Francisco's Pacific Heights district. I was greeted by a man in his early fifties, of compact build, whose thoughtful face was framed by sandy blond hair and a neatly trimmed salt-and-pepper beard. After exchanging pleasantries, we adjourned to his office. The comfortable clutter of books and papers stacked here and there gave the impression more of a scholar's study than a psychiatrist's consulting room.

Tom is a fine conversationalist, taking pleasure in an unexpected insight, a humorous observation, or an intriguing problem. Notwithstanding his impressive professional standing, he seems quite without pretense or presumption, as happy to listen as to talk. Before our meeting, I had prepared a list of questions I wanted him to address, but I soon found I had little need of it. We fell easily into our discussion, and in our rambling, we seemed to come naturally to the things I'd hoped to cover.

There was a ready match between the questions I was exploring in my writing and Tom's own lifelong interests. He has suffered long from baseball fever, as well as other sports-related maladies. He grew up in Saint Louis and, like his father, harbors a lifetime devotion to the Cardinals. As a youth, he played sports—baseball, football, tennis, basketball—at every opportunity. Like many others—like me—his love of sport wilted for several years in the turbulence of the sixties. Today, as a player, he mostly limits himself to tennis, but he is still an avid baseball fan. (A passion his wife, Jane, does not share but bravely indulges. As he tells it in the dedication in *Baseball Fever*, she once traveled with him two thousand miles to watch a World Series game, and as the teams first took the field, she turned to him and asked, "Who's playing?")

Over the course of many years, Tom has cultivated his knowledge of the inner life. As an undergraduate at Princeton he majored in philosophy and religion, graduating summa cum laude. After completing his studies at Yale Medical School, he went on to specialize in psychiatry, "that illegitimate offspring of modern medicine," as he calls it. His twin pursuits of religion and psychiatry found a home in Jungian psychology, where the tasks of transforming the spirit and healing the psyche are ever intertwined. In 1983 he completed his training as an analyst at the C. G. Jung Institute in San Francisco, and today he is a practicing analyst and chair of the institute's extended education committee.

Our first meeting took place in July 1995, a time when professional baseball was experiencing a sickness far more serious than baseball fever. The dispute between the owners and players association was choking the life out of the game, causing the cancelation of one season and the shortening of the next. The sheer ugliness of the sports business had taken center stage, and the bitterness of the intrusion had for both of us—along with millions of others—been a drain not only on our patience but also on our affection. In Tom's view, "the recent events—the strikes, the exploitative behavior, the greed and selfishness—have done damage to that line separating events on the field from the realm of ordinary concerns. It has become difficult to make that willing suspension of disbelief that is necessary to enter the world of a sport." The strike had violated that boundary between the second world and the everyday world.

The damage, should it last, would constitute a far more significant loss than is generally recognized. "The success of sport speaks of tremendous hunger for certain types of experience. Sport supplies a sense of order and simplicity, of relief from the complexities of life. It satisfies our longing for immediacy of experience, in which we use all that we have and see how it works. In this sense, play is the natural expression of the Self. And sport provides us with collective experience that has far more vitality than one finds in most situations, even in religious worship."

He pauses, but the furrowed brow suggests that the thought is not yet finished. "In natural religions," he continues, "you find the idea of the interpenetration of nature and spirit, what Jung called *lumina natura*, the light of the spirit infusing nature. One can feel this in sport. You can sense a spiritual presence in the physical acts of an athlete.

"I once heard a radio interview with Julius Erving in which he spoke of the feeling of 'leaping for God.' I had the sense that he was quite conscious of this *lumina natura*, of his physical action being lit up from within."

Tom's remarks remind me of a scene in the film *Chariots of Fire* in which the devoutly religious Scottish sprinter Eric Liddell is confronted by his equally devout sister about his decision to delay his calling as a missionary in order to compete in the 1924 Olympics. Liddell has himself harbored doubts about His decision, but he has come to recognize that running is also a divine calling: "God made me fast. And when I run I can feel his pleasure." It is an inspired statement, and an unexpected one as well. We have grown unaccustomed to the God of Abrahamic monotheism—especially in northern Protestant traditions like Liddell's—showing much concern for natural pleasures, either His own or others'. The

Song of Solomon aside, Jehovah has generally been thought to have matters more serious and pure to attend to.

The presence in sport of the Abrahamic God is certainly problematic. Why, after all, would the God who entered history to lead his chosen people out of Egypt, to redeem a fallen humanity through the suffering of his one begotten son, to seal his holy teachings through the Prophet Muhammad—why would such a God give a hoot about who wins a ball game? Are we really to suppose that God so loved the New York Giants that he delivered unto them the 1991 Superbowl by causing the Buffalo Bills' last-second field goal attempt to go wide?

The problem in all this, according to Singer, is "our failure of imagination." Unlike the ancient Greeks, we lack the reflective categories that would distinguish the workings of various agencies beyond the ego: the blustering fury of Mars exploding in the linebacker's mad charge at the quarterback, the base runner playing out Hermes' cunning trickery as he takes his lead off first, Athena's cool strategic logic guiding the coach in diagramming the last-second shot. Instead, we try to lay all divine functions at the feet of a single God, who by his very nature has little reason to concern himself with the games we play.

When Charles Barkley claims, "God is in my body," the reality of the numinous force that pours through him is difficult to refute, but the theology seems insufficient. What Barkley is describing seems closer to how Singer describes the Greek experience of athletics, which entailed "a sense of the relationship between humans and nature that is vastly different from our own." For the Greeks, the individual was seen to be energetically linked to a larger whole, comprising not just human society, "but also the plant and animal worlds, the mountains, the sky, and so forth." In this primary level of consciousness, "all things magically interrelate and participate in one another and the entire cosmos."

In our discussions, Singer frequently referred to this as the *mana* level of consciousness, a term that Jung often used. The word is Melanesian in origin, though many ancient and traditional cultures have terms with similar meaning. Jung described mana as an "extraordinary effective power emanating from a human being, object, action, or event, or from supernatural beings and spirits. Also health, prestige, power to work magic and to heal." For Jung mana was a primitive concept for the psychic energy that endows things with numinosity.

The mana level of consciousness is characterized by a primary relatedness to a world of natural powers. Mana is the vital substance, the life energy that flows through and animates all things. The consciousness that perceives this animated world is a mode of being, an inherent part of our makeup. Although it is suppressed by the causal and logical preoccupations of the rational mind, it cannot be denied. The crucial question is not whether mana consciousness will be expressed but what form its expression will take.

In Singer's view, from ancient times to the present, the immediacy of sport has evoked recognition of the presence of mana, of the vital force incarnated through action. For the ancients, this was a matter of great consequence, for mana is dynamic. "By doing something well—a sport, a dance, a ritual—one expressed one's relationship to mana, and by therefore making it move in the right direction, one participated in life's creativity."

This was not just a matter of concern for the athlete. The success of athletes signified and enhanced the virtue and vigor of the city they represented. Modern sport keeps something of this alive still today. Rally caps, mascots, cheers and waves—these are not only outlets for our enthusiasm, "They are," says Singer, "expressions of an archaic consciousness, in which symbols and magic affect the tide of events. The *polis* participates directly in the athlete's use of mana."

Throughout our discussions, Singer refers frequently to Jane Harrison's seminal study of ancient Greece, *Themis*. According to Harrison, heroes were those whose actions brought blessings by increasing the communal pool of mana. Heroism, then, was not a